RICE GRAINS
Selected Poems

Selected and Translated by
E. San Juan, Jr.

Edited by
Nan Braymer

RICE GRAINS

GRAINS

Selected Poems

AMADO V. HERNANDEZ

INTERNATIONAL PUBLISHERS   New York

Library of Congress
Catalog Card Number: 66–18280
Manufactured in the United States of America

About the Translator

Born in Manila in 1938, E. San Juan, Jr. received his B.A. from the University of the Philippines, and his M.A. and Ph.D. from Harvard University. He was a Fulbright scholar, fellow of Harvard University, and Rockefeller Foundation grantee. Previously he had been instructor of English at the University of the Philippines. Dr. San Juan is at present a teacher of English at the University of California (Davis). Author of a volume of poems, *Godkissing Carrion* (Cambridge, Mass., 1964), San Juan is also a poet in the native Tagalog and a critic of Tagalog literature. He is a contributor to many literary and scholarly journals.

Contents

Acknowledgment is due to the following periodicals in which some of the translations included in this volume first appeared: *The Asian Student, Progressive Review* (Manila), *Literature East and West, Gandhi Marg* (New Delhi), *Taliba* (Manila), and *Books Abroad.*

INTRODUCTION

Amado V. Hernandez, now in his early sixties, is the most distinguished, as well as the most significant, poet in the Philippines today. The skill and vitality of his art have exercised a profound effect on the Filipino people—primarily because there is no gap between the poet's life and his poems: experience and art are fused into a single act—that of resistance to oppression.

To understand the unique place this Filipino poet occupies, in the context of a period in which the Philippines and indeed all of Southeast Asia are caught up in a great historical crisis, it is essential to know some of the salient facts of his personal history. An ardent fighter in the cause of freedom, he was, in 1951, national president of the Congress of Labor Organizations. In the atmosphere of McCarthyism, bigotry and official corruption then prevailing, he was arrested and accused of "rebellion against the established government." Held incommunicado until his trial, he was convicted in spite of the testimony of respected civic leaders and public officials in his defense.

Hernandez was condemned to spend years of agonizing confinement in a succession of unspeakable prisons. Camp Murphy, Camp Crame, Muntinlupa, Fort McKinley, Panopio Compound—their very names symbolize the forces of death that hold the reins of domination. In the "bartolina"—the segregated dungeon—of Muntinlupa, the state prison, Hernandez wrote most of the poems included in this collection. Writing to the late Dr. Jose P. Laurel from his cell in New Bilibid Prison, July 11, 1954, Hernandez describes the travesty of due process of law, the mockery of all standards of truth and justice at his trial.

William J. Pomeroy, a valiant defender of Filipino freedom, comments in his book, *The Forest*, "The principal charge against Amado Hernandez, arrested CLO president, is that he turned a mimeograph machine over to the Huks." In the *Eastern World* of February 1954, Ralph Friedman reported the iniquities, the shameful tactics visited by the authorities on the innocent poet. The true story of the trial can still be found in the legal records and in the newspapers of the time, and they constitute a damaging indictment of his accusers.

When Magsaysay came into power in 1954, Hernandez began to be hopeful. "I feel I have also made a humble contribution to the new era on the march," he wrote. "I believe I have demonstrated how a man can suffer for his principles." But by then he seemed to have become the forgotten man. "I seem to have been abandoned," he writes. "Completely denuded of everything worth living for."

It was not until May 30, 1964, after more than six years of imprisonment and more than a decade of litigation, that the Supreme Court of the Republic finally acquitted Hernandez of the "crime of rebellion compounded with murder, arson and robbery." The case titled "People v. Hernandez" turned into a victory for Hernandez and the *true* people, whom he had always championed in word and deed. Discussing his long-drawn-out, cruel ordeal, he wrote: "The enemies of the common *tao* charged me with communistic activities because they could not charge me with dishonesty, with selling out the workers to the employers and politicians, or robbing the laborers of their legitimate earnings. . . . My conscience constantly hammers into my mind that in the life of a man there are things more precious than freedom, ambition, family and even life itself—and these are human decency and dignity."

Hernandez has survived the years of imprisonment with his spirit enriched and toughened. More vigorous than ever, he now leads the enlightened youth of the Republic. He seems to have transformed his harsh prison experience into a sacred privilege. He has set a precedent: No Filipino now can claim to be a partisan of man's freedom, of dynamic social justice in the face of an emerging police state, unless he has lived, or is prepared to live, in Muntinlupa.

In 1962, when Hernandez received the Republic Cultural Heritage Award—the highest public honor given to a man of letters in the Philippines—the judges expressed their view that his poems were of a high order, that his literary achievement was authentic— engaged, involved, committed to the world—and that his poetry "doesn't blink the facts of life, and yet it affirms the prevalence of the spirit."

This is the paradox, the tension, that energizes the complex, sometimes ambiguous, themes and forms of the poet's work. On the one hand he celebrates the everyday things and incidents: rice grains, ants, seeds, fleas, bread, dung. On the other, he dramatizes the conflicts, the rich density of human relations, as in "The Structure of Class," "Strike," and others.

Hernandez has defined a poem as "the form of the human spirit constituted by the experience, feeling, and imagination of the poet, presented through the effective use of the resources of language." In his work we see the mediating and combining function of art— the interaction of attitude and event, of phenomena and organic life. In his meditations on literature and life, he always emphasizes the role of the artist as witness to the drama of man's striving to realize his potentialities. He refuses to submit to apathetic cynicism, sentimentality, despair. The poet of a militant and outraged people cannot deny the impulse of his deepest calling—testifying to the truth of the human condition at a given historical moment.

Recently, when the city government celebrated the anniversary of the founding of Manila, Hernandez received the 1964 Manila Cultural Award for literature, with a citation that reads, in part: "In commendation of his courageous, dedicated and sustained portrayal of the social realities of our times, through his literary works in Pilipino." In response, Hernandez said: "I ascribe meaning to this honor in so far as it is a proof that the artist is directly involved, as participant and member of society, in the lot of men with whom he has been destined to live. . . . The artist is now a witness and part of the immediate present."

Hernandez, living the truth of man at a particular

period in Philippine history, finally emerges from the daemons of inward agony and outward terror—triumphant in his vision of beauty and a better life for man. At this moment, when the Republic faces with greater urgency than ever before the ordeal of finding its identity and destiny in Asia and the world; when "predatory individualism" and the exploitation of men grows more ruthless and rampant, the poems of Hernandez offer a weapon in the struggle for personal and national liberation. The poems in this book affirm the discordant realities of life and nevertheless project, in explicit sympathy with the collective spirit, an imminent breakthrough on all fronts to the fundamental exigencies of survival and happiness on earth.

E. SAN JUAN, JR.

Harvard University,
Cambridge, Massachusetts

A Man's Share of the Sky

I was betrayed by an underhand agent,
who was out to incarcerate my spirit,
thinking that because the body is frail,
human feeling and purpose could be destroyed.

I was caged up in this place of stone
and steel, gunshots, ferocious guards;
cut off from the normal world,
who counted me dead, though I still lived and
                        breathed.

At my eye's farthest reach, through that narrow
                        window,
shines my share of the sky, full of tears—
meagre solace for an injured heart,
sorry banner for a man torn up by the roots.

The guard's look is as sharp as the lightning's edge;
no one but him comes near the padlocked door;
the cry of a prisoner in a nearby cell,
sounds like an animal howling in a cave.

Daylight is a chain dragged by bloody feet,
night is a funeral shroud,
a coffin readied for a convict's grave;
the agent's claws are still felt, day and night.

Sometimes one hears the thud of footsteps,
the sound of rattling, clanking chains;
A thousand shadows are flung against the sun,
A thousand phantoms thrown out from the gloom.

Sometimes the night is shocked awake
by a siren's scream—an escape!
Blast of gunfire; sometimes a creaking bell
whimpers at the gallows: Someone's being hung.

This is my world now, it belongs to me,
this prison that is the graveyard of the living,
ten, twenty, how many years? All the years
of my life will be buried here.

But the mind fears no pain,
the heart, still steadfast, beats.
Being jailed is a part of the fight;
this kind of bondage only toughens resistance.

Neither God nor man sleeps forever, the humiliated
are not humiliated forever;
every tyrant has his day of judgment,
every Bastille has its day of vengeance.
And from here I glimpse tomorrow,
in that narrow span of sky wiped clean of tears,
foresee the rays of victory's golden dawn,
when, freed, I shall salute you, freedom.

Strike!

The work in the fields
ended.

> Machines in the factory
> halted.

>> Machines and docks
>> idled.

>>> And the people
>>> take the rap.

Investments and goods
wasting.

> Everything going to pieces,
> Strike! Strike!

>> Every stubborn,
>> stalwart soul
>> has struck.

>>> Once-oppressed minds,
>>> once-bowed heads,
>>> are lifted, erect.

The poor "little man,"
victimized,
rises up.

> Why should not
> those who plant the seed
> share the harvest?

> > He who raises
> > and roasts the pig,
> > dies of hunger.

> > > He who weaves clothes
> > > for the rich
> > > goes naked.

He who mints the coins
Must beg.

> He who built the altars
> lives in the gutter.

> > He who plows up
> > earth's riches
> > is afflicted by debt.

* * * *

But as long as there is a world
where men live like beasts,
like inhuman slaves;
as long as wages remain

mere pittance or alms;
as long as those who are exploited,
who die in harness,
suffer the pangs of hunger;
as long as getting a job
is an abasing business;
as long as the many are sacrificed
to the greed of the few;
as long as those who do not sweat,
grow fatter daily;
as long as the masters do not fear
man or God,
and crooked laws
protect the sheltered few;
the strike must come
and sow its vengeance—
the strike that has no end—
storm, fire, lightning, thunder;
the blade of an axe
that brings judgment—
until the worker's rights
are recognized, until he is redeemed
from prisons and from early graves;
until labor, the new Christ
nailed on the cross,
is risen once more.

(In part)

The Ant

O noble ant, halt a while
while I pay
homage to you.

Your power lies
in the possession
of all the virtues,
your wisdom is that of
Solomon.

With each grain you bear,
your endless work
proceeds
with maximum
velocity.

You attack the loads
of sundry ruins,
you tear down
fort and mountain.

Working together
as long as the light lasts
each move you make with your comrades
leads to the massive mound you build.

What you plan
and initiate,
you push yourself to do
to the limit of your power.

How enduring your bond
with others!
You'll fight
against foes
until you are crushed.

Compared
to other insects
you, O offspring of toil,
will be studied,
by the people of the world.

If men
would only learn from you,
this world
would be remade.

The Machine

Progress took on Mercury's wings
after man discovered fire,
after man invented the wheel;
the turtle was left far behind; revolution
kept pace with the rumble of industry.

Labor in fields, in factory, in home,
that once relied on human hands,
now is accelerated, intensified
through the miracle of the machine,
everything tends to multiply and prosper.

Jungles are cleared, mountains leveled;
fallow fields turn fertile; barren soil is plowed;
printing arrives;
land, water and air are conquered:
what man has wrought is a challenge to God!

By chance we seem to have discovered those things
that were able to improve the conditions of our lives;
but simultaneously
we fashioned weapons of war,
and men became the destroyers of men!

Electricity, radio, the atom—the magic
of all modern artifacts;
the sun of capitalism penetrating everywhere
and becoming in the clear light
the most efficient killer of man.

Because the machine became property
that could be captured—like land, like money—
we saw machines enslaving men,
instead of being their deliverers.

How heavy the cost of the Machine, our Lord,
as man becomes a buffalo with a rope through his nose!
O civilization,
when will the apocalypse arrive
on earth, when will man assert his dominion?

O man, freedom is tied to the stake,
only your hands can liberate her.
The time is ripe for
all gray spirits to perish. Is it God or the Machine
that enchains you, child of Prometheus?

One World

A war ended
like the explosion
  of a firecracker
  on New Year's eve.

The tears and blood
were not yet dry
  when the nations
  again exploded in war.

One world was to have been
built—
  a Shangri-la
  of democracy.

The first steps
were taken:
  but the promised union
  soon split in partisanship.

Like a rice-cake
split in two
  were Germany
  and Korea.

India-Pakistan
a severed twin,
    and Indo-China
    a fruit cut up.

Gigantic China
and tiny Taipeh
    Like Goliath and David
    sharpening blades.

Rapidly the gulf
grows now
    between the East
    and the West.

One world?
What a dream!
    what is the mission
    of the atomic bomb?

Maybe the universe
will be united
    if Christ
    should come again.

A Poem on Poetry

Like God:
there is a poem in all things—
the dawn as fragrant as a chosen bride,
the beauty of night where darkness gleams;
in the fields, life; in cities, music.

Like God:
those who can recognize a poem are rare,
diamond is often taken for carbon,
the sky is seen as reflected in ditch-water,
the outlaw's a patriot and the patriot a fraud.

Like Man:
a poem is created by one who is also a god;
the mind of the poet often performs miracles—
a few coarse-grained words, apprehended,
become bullets and roses.

Like Man:
a poem bears its own measure, melody, rhythm,
the three elements of its loveliness;
and freedom is the wing of a poem
that makes it soar.

Like God:
a poem is a unique riddle whose answer
lies in the throb of each sentient heart,
it is riches in poverty, brilliant light in darkness,
and pure honey in the bitter poison.

Like Man:
it is a rocky mountain and a nugget of gold,
a camel that passes through the needle's eye . . .
the true poem is an arrow
that pierces the target it chooses point-blank!

The Bill Collector

A knock on the door. "Who's there?"
  "It's the bill collector, Ma'am."
  No answer.
He repeats the knock until the door
quietly gives way . . . A voice says: "Come in . . ."
The bill collector stands there thunderstruck,
retreats as though struck by a cobra,
                    his eyes pop out,
the rent bill flutters to the floor,
as the naked woman comes toward him.

Vow for Freedom's Sake

I was imprisoned by the enemies of freedom—
I fought for freedom from hunger, fear, and for the
liberty to speak,
to worship God and to reject false idols.
Thanks, a thousand thanks.
I know I am not alone . . .
Tens, hundreds, thousands, millions—victims of a
like fate—
will be the inheritors of a glorious tomorrow.

* * * *

The thousands degraded in prisons,
whose innocence, like mine, has made them guilty;
the thousands tortured and persecuted
with neither trial nor verdict in an honorable court.
The countless ones
who have been victimized
in fields and villages, in cities and in towns;
in hovels and tenements gutted by fire
how many living souls were buried without names,
without a cross?
We will not forget, they will not be forgotten,
their voices reach the ears of tomorrow's avengers.

* * * *

Yes, my body is imprisoned,
but the darting mind and the throbbing heart
will never be made captive by steel or gold;
my dreams and my thoughts,
together with the free wind and the sun's light,
the bird's chirping, the wave's tumult, the
                                    bullet's rumble,
in the protest of the people against betrayal, against
                                    senseless orders,
in man's vow to fight the leaders without conscience,
                                    who thrive on evil;
my soul that knows no weariness will go with them,
till my country gains its own pure promised land—
and though they crack my skull, and even kill me—
on my skull, engraved in raw blood, they will read:
"This is a Filipino who never would surrender
            to the brutish enemies of freedom."

(*In part*)

The Kingdom of Mammon

The boulevards burn with violence
in the furious swarm of electric lights;
and in the avenues, turtle-wise,
hordes of cars roar with fierce energy.

Buildings that tower with arrogance
in Escolta have turned into rows of grave-stones;
who will want or crave from the markets
fruits and goods that have grown rotten?

On every side there's pleasure and distraction,
fiesta and dancing, night-long, day-long;
radios, newspapers, shops, hotels,
all serve every whim of "high society."

Our country is so progressive and prosperous—
that's what the tourists are impressed by;
who dares whisper that thousands have no roofs
above their heads; that hunger stalks this town?

The Skull of the King

King Philip was a Napoleon in his time,
he became lord of petty Macedonia
and other lands that could not resist his armies.

When he died, his son became even mightier,
As Alexander the Great he was the conqueror
of all Europe and Asia, laid low by his armies.

Alexander had the notion he would glorify his father,
the dead king, and so he opened up his grave,
wanting to bury treasures with the warrior's bones.

There he beheld a heap of skulls, of skeletons
                             embracing.
The Emperor became confused:
How should he divide the treasure—
how much to the king, how much to his thousand
                                  slaves?

Just Before Dawn

The black pit is suddenly flung open
in this burial place of the living—
the Leader arrives, fiery eyes burning,
voice booming out the fateful words:
"If you wish to regain your freedom,
You have only to sign this—"

The piece of paper, shaped like a diploma,
was flung to the floor, lay there safely
till the condemned man, skeletal and gaunt,
picked it up, tore it to bits in fury
as sudden as the lightning flash that struck him.

Before the dawn unfurls its light,
the hapless convict is led out by soldiers,
led out to Nowhere . . .
Suddenly the darkness is shattered
by the sun soaked in blood.

Rice Grains

Man and the water buffalo have been companions from
                                                    the beginning,
Industry and strength naturally fuse;
                    the wilderness of thorns
is cleared by the far-ranging plow,
                    the fields are tilled,
the upturned soil is harrowed.

Rain and warmth in turn bestow
blessings upon the purified soil,
                    after a week,
fat seeds are spilled on earth,
and after that a million little spears wave at the sky.

When the stems rise to the span of two fingers,
the plants are ranged in rows and ranks;
                                as it grows,
palay becomes an emerald sea;
                when the wind swirls,
the fields turn into green, waving hair.

Together the womb of the mother and the earth
are plowed and sowed;
                when palay
burgeons, after warm nurturing,
                life responds, too,
in the swelling breasts of the caring mother.

After nine months of growing,
the grains of the stalks burn ripe;
                            the stems
bow down with a teeming load.
        Beneath the mother's heart
the secret can no longer be concealed.

Palay is reaped; the bales of gold
lie about on the joyful abundant earth,
                            muscles that defy
fatigue, soon heap and bind
                    the bales,
piling them up in towering mounds.

How bountiful is the harvest,
the joy of lovers in the dear fruit of their loins!
                            a happy baby
is born out of the bodies of mother and father . . .
                        O, predestined season
when man and palay are as twins.

Before Christmas, the child is christened;
how fragrant is the cooked rice on the table,
                    the newly-pounded grains,
puddings and cakes and every kind of sweet.
                        Out of this soil
come the beauty and the hard reality of life.

The Worker Hero

I am a worker: one grain of the sands
that fill up the ruts, but also build the temples.
Perhaps I owe my life to God,
but my lot is a debt to myself.
I know the law: "Man, from your own sweat
you will earn your daily bread."

*   *   *   *

I erected Greece and Rome,
I destroyed arrogant Troy:
my hands are hammers, weapons to create
and destroy at will.
If you see before you any products of labor,
It was I who shaped them, gave them birth.

*   *   *   *

I am the monarch without throne or crown,
a master who must always obey another.
How many lucky men have I helped enrich,
while I myself remained hungry?
How many stood upon my shoulders?
My orphans have become Mammon and Nabob . . .

*   *   *   *

. . . All the buildings, streets and vehicles
were wrought by my hands of steel;
by the power I discovered—oil, coal, iron—
industry and commerce performed miracles;
but the gap between my life and property
widened . . . and my life has been subjugated.

* * * *

To deprive my person of dignity
was the work of scheming minds;
but gold will indubitably remain gold,
fragrance of earth will elude concealment;
and if I am negated by the corruptors,
who will deny the final judgment of history?

(In part)

Earth

I was christened
by the enemy,
stripped naked of name and liberty;
Ravished
in a cruel cage, on this lonely rock.

Cold, this rock-cradle
of pain,
for a weakened heart it is like the clutch of the grave.
No intrusion here
of wind, sunlight—and no dawn.

Tears nourished me,
The earth was my mat, in turn, too hot, too cold;
how dark the sky
shrouded by a thousand sorrows in the night!

With pain beyond endurance,
I saluted
the power of noble earth.
What miracle is this?
Heart and soul cried out at this Promethean power.

I am vowed
To vigil;
Earth is the beginning of all things,
Out of it come
the seed of green hope and life's ripening.

The Blacksmith

A lump of iron ore pried out of the mountainside
yields to the fire's touch until it softens;
then after patient hammering in the forge,
it is molded by the smith to his heart's desire.

A moment passes—and a tool emerges,
the lump of ore turns into a steel plough;
it turns up the soil with fierce energy,
to the rhythms of sowing, under the blessing of rain.

Then one day revolt blazes up,
the whole country is a fiery volcano,
the true patriots organize an army
to direct the battle's unleashed rage.

Swiftly the old plough is made white-hot again,
the burning edge is forged anew:
it turns into a blade that seems to vow
vengeance for the injuries of a people.

A piece of steel, and yet it does not glitter,
its value never can be measured—
Forged into a plough it helps to nourish all!
Forged into a sword it is the anvil of the land!

Look upon the blacksmith, solid as steel,
humbly quiet in his corner;
for in his work-stained hands he holds
life, liberation and his nation's selfhood.

Beyond all Riches

He who once was rich grew poor and wept,
    the sky looked ragged in the gutter's mire;
his name that was a flower on men's tongues,
    vanished with all its fragrance in the night.

Now no more wealth, no more praise and glory,
    the goals he strove for all his living days.
In faith and in repentance,
    now the only thing he longs for is: a friend.

According to Darwin

The little boy saw the monkey in the garden:
   "Why without clothes?" was his question;
the father, who had studied Darwin,
   answered his child without delay:

"If you dressed that ape
   and put him in a flashy car . . .
just think what a scandal there would be
   if he were called an honorable Congressman!"

Sodom

A society of phony sophistication and artifice—
that's the Hesperides
of the fortunate—an oasis
in the misery that surrounds it:
In the king's house,
a ladder climbing to the rainbow
is planted in the gutter;
in the priest's house,
up and down go the pale, smooth legs;
an iron hand gloved in silk,
muddy feet shod in gold;
a niche, bright and flowery,
guards skull and skeleton;
eyes and mouth electrical
dominate the earth and sky;
but in the Tower of Babel
of one who flees from himself,
there is a new Sanhedrin,
the judge himself—the perfect criminal.
This social set is given to drunkenness,
blood is the wine of its amusement.
Ah, this is Society,
a fig tree whose root is rotted;
silver is the skin
of the tiny mullet,
with progress learned from the crab,
with the watchfulness of the blind;
a golden watch in the bracelet

does not tell the time of the vanished nights and days;
these humans are drunk under their glittering façades,
unaware of their soul's gaping wounds;
seduced by the fanfare proclaiming
their supreme condition,
they are deaf to the sobs and cries
of the hungry, the victims;
they indulge in flights to the clouds,
but are unable to read the handwriting—
the hands of lightning
pointing to the last hour!

The Road (I)

On this day I look back,
for I have traveled far—
   a half-century,
shouldering the cross to Calvary
without even one Simon Cyrene.

Only a summer ago I was an innocent child,
Miracles teemed in my sight and my mind,
   then the sun pivoted,
December came with its sharp, cold bite—
the world is not always in the April season.

On a ladder to the promised land, I followed
   the rainbow,
   till I knew
that all the fantasies of the heart are rainbows:
if looked at from afar, the sky, if touched, ashes.

Once a Prometheus, I brought fire
to the wounded in the darkness;
   I was punished
by the vindictive gods who cried out,
"The light of Olympus is not for creatures of clay!"

I found at times, as Florante did,
that wickedness often rules,
   and good is often downed;
and then I tried to give virtue its due:
I turned into Don Quixote tilting at windmills.

How rare the man who doesn't act like the shrimp,
flowing along with the tide, getting what it needs;
   the wise serpent
imitates the color of grass and wood;
the bird in the cage still is a bird that sings.

So many tangled paths in the world,
more destruction than one had dreamed of,
   everywhere lurks a demon—
at the starting place, sand leads to the sea;
a lake stretches out to the jungle.

One Who Died Twice

A close embrace that could not be loosened,
A thousand inexhaustible kisses,
the promises of two hearts pressed close
could not be loaded in a hundred jeeps.

This man was a soldier going off to war,
a bug who had leaped into the fire;
the sweetheart, left behind, to face the fact
that call of country ranked ahead of love.

When months like a necklace of sighs
had passed, the soldier met his end;
the widowed sweetheart got the message:
"Your beloved has perished."

One afternoon, a woman in mourning,
visited a church;
her hair was silver, her face gray as lead,
tears poured forth as she crossed herself.

With deep sorrow, she kneeled before the altar,
"God, have mercy on my son . . ."
While outside the church, in a jeep,
the girl who was bereaved
waits in the arms of another soldier.

The Road (II)

All roads are both good and evil,
all prayers are heard by God;
    to step on earth
is to fulfill your destiny, your longed-for goal,
to tread on wind is to lose your way.

In the flowery beauty of my chosen road,
I learned how to withstand temptation;
    I also realized
that intelligence, not convention, is the key
to the door of life, whether sad or glorious.

And now, in my last journey,
when the black frontier is only a few steps away,
    on my grave,
you will read my history:
"He did not follow the old trodden ways."

The Soldier and the Huk

Like a crack of thunder resounded
the meeting of the soldier and the Huk—
                    the final reckoning!
like a volcano, the fire within,
the gathered hate,
erupt . . .

Both prepare with the fervor
of patriotic heart and arms of steel;
                    both in hot pursuit
of triumph for their cause,
armored in daring and conviction.

They penetrate the jungle, harrow the plain,
climb the mountains, ransack the far-flung fields,
                    not a sound,
shadow and smoke were left behind;
they have the lion's will to kill or be killed.

Seventeen days were blackly buried,
seventeen nights darkness shrouded
                    even the stars;
but the soldier and the "criminal" Huk,
  lay waiting for their weapons to cross.

Dusk crept in on a melancholy air,
with wind and rain and a sky torn by lightning;
                                    at last,
at the edge of the ravine in the darkness,
two bolos suddenly flashed.

Before long the storm subsided,
the moon glimpsed, as it silvered over all the debris,
                              the terrifying shapes,
at the edge of the ravine,
two dying men, gasping for life.

The Huk and the soldier had met at last,
embracing each other in death;
            the moon wept . . .
for at the last moment they both knew
they were brothers who had been torn asunder.

The Firefly

You will live only through this night,
tiny jewel
offered to the beauty
of the eternal evening;
tomorrow you're sure to be a little corpse, a teardrop
from my lamentation, on the face of a flower.

Bread

He had been imprisoned
for so many years,
time was a chain around his neck
knotted up in the windings of his life.

A piece of bread
and a can of broth
are left at the door by the guard,
he grabs them with dirty hands.

When the wretched man
is about to swallow,
the tear-soaked bread drops,
rubbing against the bruise in his heart.

He remembers why
he was imprisoned:
he stole a box of crackers
because his sick child was groaning with hunger.

Trying to get away
from the fist of the law,
he killed his pursuer—
and never saw his little girl again!

Now life wears away
wearily, though now every day
he is given the bread that might have saved
his child, who died of hunger.

The Hand

Observe carefully our world:
fields, factories, streets, statues,
earth, sea, sky have been dominated
by the hands of men, which can move mountains.

I too trained my hands for expert work,
to prepare for the hard days ahead;
how ugly my words woven in silk,
compared to the hands of the worker mining gold.

My hands, oh dearest love, were
like flowers, clean and fragrant;
and when I am ill or in danger,
the touch of your hand is healing balm.

And all the while the hands of the clock,
point to the prophetic mouth:
"Man, all of you will meet the end
decreed by this—time's hand."

Rendezvous with God

I have looked everywhere for God,
from the time I was a child,
I've pursued a thousand paths
through the clearings of the years,
I've consumed a ton of delicious herbs.
At the end of the trail I would see a
flash, then it was gone—just a distant light,
a firefly in the April night.

Frustrated, yet victorious,
victorious, yet dismayed,
embraced by virtue and clasped by honor,
I soon discovered that honor and virtue are coquettes.
I tasted the world's rejection, was stripped of
                              everything,
learned how to smile at bitter loss,
to guard the sweetest moment lest it be poisoned,
to learn that life's wounds must be worn as medals or
                              blossoms.
(Diamonds are most costly when they have been
                    abraded on every facet.)
In my despair—
living-dying in spirit and heart,
the flame of conviction
still persisted,
searching, tracking, inquiring
in whatever time or place,
the God of peoples

the God of nations
the God of all creation.

*   *   *   *

I walked the fields,
the soil of affliction of the unnamed oppressed;
the muddy paths are hard to follow,
the feet fear splinter and mire
on the way to the grave-mounds of poverty
flung among the dry weeds.
I asked
and was shocked at the harsh answer,
savage and fiery.
For in my heart,
flickers the fear
that they have long since changed their horizons,
that the anguish of endurance has killed all hope;
hunger, sickness, debt
inherited forever;
whenever land, dearly loved, is tilled,
like the monster's jaw,
it bites the benefactor.
Have they been renounced by God?
Then they will put their fates in the hands of another
god—

justice is its name
justice rice clothing house land
reason rights liberty liberation—
the claim of a life staked out.

*   *   *   *

Where?
What place
does God inhabit?
what heaven and what continent?
What wilderness, rocky shore or mountain?
What field, sky or summit?
In what temple and altar, tabernacle or monument?
What lands have I not roamed?
What others have I not flown over
in the flight of dreams?
What fancies, what fantasies, what illusions?
Where's God?
Why doesn't he answer?
Has he forgotten man?
Has he fallen asleep in Aphrodite's lap?
Has he no defense against Circe's enchantment?
Dante, Virgil, guide me
to Utopia
to Nirvana
to Shangri-la
to Olympus or the empyrean!

*   *   *   *

. . . because I am of Adam,
child of sin;
belief and doubt
are twins at birth;
the days dropped off like withered leaves, men
                               withered too;
winter with its bluster blights the spring,
the procession of seasons cannot be stopped.

In my mind the memory of what has gone,
returns and lives.
Now is my twilight filled with sorrow,
hands wrinkled, hair ash-gray,
blurred eyesight, heart that refuses to throb . . .
now, suffused with longing, kneeling
at the feet of a cross,
I cry God, God, God!
Silence alone answers
louder than a volcano's thunder.

One sorrowful night,
all things, the very stars, weep,
tears shine like meteors,
the spirit is drained of faith and hope,
life is a pale flash struggling through my agony,
choking in the scornful dark.

. . . I heard a voice
speaking to my own spirit and mind:
. . . "You searched for Me
hunted in every corner of the world
except in your heart and soul.
. . . I am your conscience."

A smile stirred on my lips,
I felt like a silly butterfly
who had flitted about
looking for loveliness and delicious scents,
and only when its wings were clipped recalled
that its wings are the twin petals of a flower.

O God
I am you and you are me
that which I pursued all the days of my life
in the far corners of the earth
lived all the while in the substance of my own heart!

(In part)

Two Questions

In life there is an ordinary question
whose answer is the key
to the door between being and not-being,
between acceptance and rejection,
between selfhood and slavehood.

When a man's thirst for knowledge is too easily
                                              assuaged,
it would be well
to examine the real value of what he lives by:
though he may be informed,
he may not be free.

But if he asks the important question
as to the nature of things,
persisting till he gets the answer
that opens the way to objective truth,
then he is a free spirit who measures the sky.

Forbidden

On his knees
the villainous sentry of the fortress
speaks to God
makes the sign of the cross,
makes responses to the priest's prayers,
follows these with "Amen Jesus."

Amid the crowd of the faithful, I saw my only child,
the jewel of my heart, praying.
The awkward eight-year-old kneeling in prayer,
through parched lips telling his rosary:
"Our Father,
give us back our father."

His heart's wound is written in the hollows of his eyes,
he has been stabbed by seven daggers,
and in the failing light,
I see, with bitter pain,
this sweet child,
gnawed like a rosebud, blighted by the worm
of hunger and disease.

When the mass and the prayers were over,
my son looked back and saw me,
possessed by hope
I waved to my cherished child,
torn out of my heart and life
by a lying world

and a stone-blind judge.
My boy tried to rush into my waiting arms.

Come, o, my child,
I call out timidly,
holding out my arms like joyful wings
for my son, the only cure for my grief.

But the guard,
kneeling on the cushion with head bowed, crosses
                                    himself
with eyes like the glint of an axe-blade,
turns on my son and me, blazing with anger.
How abruptly he forgets God,
but never, even once, the duty
the king has imposed on him.
Forbidden!
I am quickly turned about.

The iron door is open, then shut tight,
my child has vanished out of sight,
has been driven away,
without our ever embracing
even for a few mute seconds.
He never put his skinny arms around my neck,
and out of my heart, seething with grief,
I had no chance to share a little warmth with him.
My body dries out, becomes diseased in this
                                    confinement,
the door clangs shut, my child may never return,
my eyes feel struck by lightning,
curses lie on my dry lips.

The wind outside my cell sobs,
brings me the echo of a vanishing voice,
the phantom of a kiss drenched in tears of love,

I am a useless stump abandoned
dead-alive
in the dreadful gloom of prison.
New chains of foreboding have been laid on me:
my son has been abandoned
to fight a stormy sea alone.
How bleak his present life,
his future wrapped in darkness.
A year, five, ten—his whole life!
My entire being
is swallowed into an abyss as wide as an open grave,
I am felled by a thousand deaths,
while in my soul, without end,
there comes the echo of the word:
forbidden, forbidden, forbidden.

The Structures of Class

When a few men establish
a government to rule the life of many,
they lay down rules, choose leaders, pass laws,
construct machines to implement their power;
embody their principles in a constitution,
decide on the balance of power, the values and the
scales.
All this is devised and ordered in accord with their own
interests,
as they control everyone's comings and goings.

Although it would be rational to suppose
that the wisest policy is justice—
equality for all in an association of brothers—
what happens is the very opposite
and to the man who sees clearly, the world is upside
down.
The few who organized these institutions
take care to reserve the privilege for their class, signing
away the heritage of all others.
"There you are, and here we are"—a king's decree
proclaims the boundary lines, the limits of class.

In time, cities arise,
places of learning hold up a golden torch,
he who would gather knowledge must enter these
doors,
but few can pass without a loaded purse,

and once inside, their minds will be exposed
to those who, void of warmth, in all their arrogance,
will try to warp even the purest heart,
and burn incense to their own brand of dubious hero.

They build a place of worship,
a temple "dedicated to God,"
setting up an image with a woman's face, a lion's body;
whoever fails to worship and pay her tribute, will never
                                         get to heaven.
Men are completely terrorized,
made to believe there was no heaven on earth, only
                                         crosses to bear.
Those who long for mysterious redemption
must give riches and land to Mammon,
must buy even immortality with prayers and gold.

For those who are determined to be absolute rulers,
good faith, tradition, a people's history are not needed.
Courthouses are built, judges and officials with no
                                         semblance of heart are chosen.
The character of the defendant is no part of judgment;
while biased justice says that equal punishment will be
                                         meted out, according to law,
it casts a net from which the big fish escape, in which
                                         the little fish are caught,
and mercy can be bought with silver.

The crowning infamy
of this law of "tooth for tooth"
is prison—that desolate cavern,

that living grave for men of health and courage—
                  equally with villains and imbeciles—
here the vengeance, the fear and hatred
of society, is centered in all its ferocity,
here one without guilt toward man or God is tortured,
and prison is a fortress of horror
where hangmen wreak havoc in the dark and
                        undermine reason.

Now, when the day of judgment comes,
and the mighty have been leveled;
(but only if the persecuted open their eyes,
only if they arise and sweep away the few)
the edifice of privilege will crumble,
and in the ashes a new temple will arise;
a new rampart, a new flag, a trumpet of promise
that the nation will grow, out of the people's hope, out
                     of their faith in their own leaders.